Kaspar Hauser

Kaspar Hauser

Europe's Child.
Why not the World's?

David Donaldson

Wynstones
Press

Published by
Wynstones Press
Stourbridge
England.

www.wynstonespress.com

First edition 2025

Cover illustration by David Newbatt.

Printed in UK.

ISBN 978-1-915416-05-6

Contents

Preface

The enigma of Kaspar Hauser has as much to say about the nature of human beings and of evil, as it does about Kaspar himself. In Jakob Wassermann's novel of 1908, Kaspar is described as *the glorious image of the divine*, through the fictional creation of Clara. It seems it was not possible for him to take this perspective from Kaspar's foremost witnesses and guardians who expressed similar views, because each contributed through their human foibles and weaknesses to Kaspar's downfall and eventual murder in a world where such a thing was only to be expected. Her astute prophecy that *he will be as mighty in death as he was powerless in life* is surely tempered by the fact that she herself is overcome by her own passion for the truth she sees in Kaspar, goes mad and never recovers her sanity.

How does Wassermann's fictional take on the story, square with the human characters we meet in their reports, observations and first hand experiences of Kaspar? True, none of them are 'perfect' but they were open to recognising and being inspired by the extraordinary human/angelic qualities Kaspar displayed. Whatever their failings, their recognition was crucial to Kaspar being 'rehabilitated' to the extent that became possible in a world where both conventional pedagogy and diet were inimical to his pristine nature.

In sharp contrast, there were those like Police Counsel Friedrich Merker who suspected Kaspar from the start, the first in a long line of sceptics hostile to all he was observed to be by those most closely engaged with looking after him, a polarisation that has continued to this day.

If we then consider 'glasses half-full or half empty', I imagine Wassermann would have viewed the likes of Daumer and Feuerbach, for example, for all their good intentions, as half empty. Yet if Kaspar had fallen into other hands, like those of his confirmed sceptics, he would have been, if not 'hung in the chimney', then put into some institution and forgotten. Or– would he? If those same people had actually had the face to face contact with him that they so conspicuously lacked? No, the glasses of the likes of Daumer were at least half-full and capable of being filled further so long as they retained that sense of a human being as more than the evolved higher animal of the nineteenth century.

At the onset of the Industrial Revolution, despite all the grotesque and evil attempts to suppress it, a bright star shone out in Central Europe, a sort of counter-force to the materialism increasingly dominating people's outlooks. Kaspar's political destiny may have been brutally suppressed but the essential human/divine spirit so clearly witnessed by Pastor Fuhrmann has continued to shine ever since despite all attempts to defame it. In this sense, the tragedy enacted around this individual and the 'unrealised history' that can be traced through the succeeding centuries down to the present, if recognised from a spiritual point of view, transforms into a seed containing the fullness of our potential human future along with the clearest indications of the forces opposing that future. As Karl Heyer concludes in his seminal study of Kaspar Hauser, it is this 'future promise that we must focus on'.

There gleam like stars
In the heaven of eternal being
The God-sent Spirits.
May all human souls
In earthly evolution
Glimpse their flame of light.

(Rudolf Steiner, quoted in
Kaspar Hauser: The Struggle for the Spirit by Peter Tradowsky)

Prologue: Setting the Scene

The Imperial Way

Kaspar is born on 29th September 1812.
Napoleon has invaded Russia and has
reached Moscow by 14th September.

Superman. His emblematic Bee
Has turned to monstrous Wasp
Unable to forgo its lethal sting.

On he presses into futility and
Moscow burning. The three-fold
Revolution's reduced to passion

Yoked to tyranny. In retreat
He meets his nemesis: foreshadows
The future in the winter snows.

Old ways are being recast. New
Furnaces for industrial might.
New horizons to contemplate:

Human beings humbled, earth-
Bound, of primate origins. *Liberty*,
Equality, *Fraternity*, not quite dead

Along with the countless slain
But limping on (and held in check)
By reason of *The Survival of the Fittest*.

Doctrine to stiffen the industrial spine
Of rival Empires bidding for sway
In the Imperial way.

Rising Wealth

Man has closed himself up till he sees
all things through the narrow chinks
in his cavern. W. Blake

c.1815

For many, their World's fallen
Off a cliff. How can they find
The means to live? That One,

Led astray by sheer force
Of genius, shipped out of
Harm's way into the Atlantic,

What difference does it make?
Rising wealth's much deadlier.
What peace for the enslaved?

Or for cottage workers
Displaced, pitched headlong
Into smoke and airless slums?

Capital turns desperation
To remorseless use; sets
Little children labouring

Beneath unguarded machines.
What Brave New World
Is this, wrapped in black,

A shroud,
    a dense descending
        suffocating cloud?

The Year without a Summer

1816

The bright sun was extinguis'd,
Writes Byron…*the icy Earth*
Swung blind and blackening
In the moonless air…no love was left…

To compete with equal horror,
John, his personal physician,
Unleashed *The Undead, the Vampire*,
Compelled to seek out human blood;

While Mary Shelley dreamt of bits
Of corpses reassembled by
Fantastical science and there!
Frankenstein was raised to life.

Entertainment? Maybe. Needing
To wile away enforced seclusion,
Holidaying by Lake Geneva
During *the year without a summer*.

Imprisoned by the weather, their
Challenge and inspiration was
To match the eerie atmosphere,
Its cold and dark, its storms,

Its torrential rain. Unseasonal
Natural Causes giving rise
To unnatural Spiritual Effects?

Mt. Tambora

April 1815

Every natural Effect has a Spiritual Cause (W. Blake)

Like molten lava, the upwelling revolutionary
Ferment streaming across Europe. In its wake
Trailed an ashen veil from distant Mt. Tambora.

It darkened the sun, cooled the atmosphere.
Famine followed as harvests failed. Families
Became refugees, scoured the countryside

Searching for food. Such *the year without a summer*,
Which inconvenienced those by Lake Geneva,
Stirred up their underworlds with tales

Of abiding horror. The One bestriding Europe,
Had brought death instead of healing.
For *Freedom*, *Fraternity*, revolutionary frenzy blazed,

Itself reduced to ash at Waterloo. How twined,
How inter-related our misguided depths
With Earth's own seething elemental unrest?

Schloss Beuggen

1815

Intended as a field hospital
In the wars of liberation.
But the locals kept well clear.

An epidemic of typhus
Had turned it into a charnel house.
Three thousand were buried here.

It overlooks the Rhine
Downstream from Laufenburg.
One arrow slit of a window

In a cellar room admits
This view, though wooden slats
Could close out all but

The merest chinks of light.
Darkness reigned, as Byron
Was to write. *No love was left…*

Continued over…

How visible the wall painting
Of a small horse in fading red?
Token gesture to entertain

The infant captive here,
Imprisoned victim of a pitiless
Dynastic shadow play,

Entangled microcosm
In the heart of World-
Upheavals. Lies sown to wind

About the stem of Truth,
Create a twilight murk.
In place of one given out

For dead, usurping Powers
Rule instead.

The Experiment

A crime against the soul life of the human being
(Anselm Ritter von Feuerbach)

c. October 1816

A message in a bottle pleading (in Latin)
On behalf of a prisoner held nearby;
Cast into the Rhine near Laufenburg
As if its fate lay with Providence to decide.

Once fished out and the news had spread,
The cellar-dungeon was vacated. Another
Cell awaited in Pilsac near Nuremberg,
This time, the treatment diabolically

More harsh: the infant caged in a tiny space
Unable to stand upright. What manner
Of crime was this, even in a glut of war?
Drive him away or hang him in the chimney.

From words he was unwittingly to deliver
Years later, once released to stumble
Blindly into the World. Who was this child?
To be so crippled in body, mind and soul?

What manner of threat was he perceived
To be to a Status Quo of ruling Powers,
Shaken to the foundations
of their entrenched control?

1. *Imprisonment and Release*

Stolen at birth. Treated with care
Until around the time his memory
Begins to stir. Then caged, unable
To stand. All prior development set
Into reverse. Childhood, a stupor
Of sleep and waking. Eyes never
Coming to focus a world beyond
Shades of darkness. Sun, moon,
Stars, the green earth, another's
Human form, unknown to memory.
His world, a shuffling to and fro
Between sitting and lying; a hand
At times reaching over his from behind
To guide the spelling of his name,
A man's voice speaking it and some
Words of dialect. Two wooden horses
For play. A diet of bread and water.
Life and death held in perpetual
Suspense. The soul-spirit unable
Either to unfold or die. Planned
Cul-de-sac. An ailing new-born
Days old (and soon to be despatched)
To take the vacant place. Hushed
Conspiracy. The perfect crime.

At 16, the wrecking treatment's judged
Complete, his destiny buried beyond
Recovery. He will be released as one
Re-ordered to disappear into the world
Without a trace: be taken on in pity
As a stable-hand or disposed of as too
Retarded to be of use. He's pulled out.
Hoisted to his feet. Given leave to stand,
An agony of swaying, tottering, stumbling,
Falling flat; thrust into the blaze of day,
Devoid of concepts: green, grass, trees;
All a blur of mounting terror. Far rather
Those quiet shades of darkness.
But the man's insistent and has
To be obeyed: to stand, walk, bear
The overwhelm of light, the insufferable
Green. Leave behind the grey womb
Of incarceration, its perpetual half-light,
Its mists of absence, its vacant dreams

Tallow Square, Nuremberg, 4.00pm

Whit Monday 26th May 1828

Released at Whitsun.
Copious religious tracts
In his pockets. Why?
For mockery? Lurch
Forward, Pentecostal fire
Of forty words of dialect
And incoherent notes
About wanting to be
A rider like his father!

Wreckage truly wrought
On *Kaspar Hauser;*
More than worldly hands
At work on the matter.
His first name that of
The dark king bearing myrrh
For the Christ-child,
The future's suffering
And sacrifice foretold.

And to first appear
In *Tallow Square!* His light
Snuffed out leaving him
This melted puddle of himself,
Notes in hand, (all proven
Forgeries, tissues of lies),
Abandoned to his fate,
In pain from each placed
Footstep, each swaying

Movement of the hips.

*

Sun's torturing brightness. Terror
Striking from the clock tower. One arm
Extended like a scarecrow's, a letter
Thrust between stiff stick fingers.

Two shoemakers approach.

He's no understanding of their questions,
Keeps on repeating nonsense. But one
Letter indicates the Riding Master's Stables.
They're close by. He's led there and has

To wait. Would he like a plate of meat?
Some beer? The smell's enough to arouse
Disgust. All he wants is bread, water
And oblivion.

From the Riding Master to the Police

He's roused when the Master arrives.
But what's this? Impulsive fascination
At the Master's uniform. The shining fabric.

The arrested child, reaching to feel and fondle,
Oblivious to this, his first job interview.
The Master steps away repelled. Can't make

Anything of the letters. Decides to pass him on
To the police. The journey there could be
One of the Stations of the Cross though he's

Only himself to carry: the agony of unused
Feet, frail legs and hips. He keeps repeating
His jumble of words, a piteous appeal

Of incoherence, as if reaching out in self-
Defence. In the police station, a candle flame
Draws him close. He reaches to touch then

Bursts into a fit of tears at the unexpected
Scorch. Exchange of looks, raised eyebrows.
What have we here? Who is he? Can he write?

All eyes on the piece of paper, as he sits
To his first scholastic test and writes down
'Kaspar Hauser'. That's better. In conclusion,

The police decide on the town gaol. To spare
His agony, he's carted there, finds himself
In a cell with a boy to question him. Dim

Grey light, sacks of straw, imprisoning walls
Of stone. It's more like home. Before
The questioning can begin, he's settled down,

Curled up, fast asleep.

Kaspar is Examined

28th May 1828

He can't be understood. At first his gibberish
Invites *harsh treatment*, suspicion. Is he mad?
Is he a fraud? All he can do is sob and sob.
It's painful to watch: mouth wide open,
Lower jaw protruding, the animal dullness
Of his face.
Two days later, the State
Medical Officer, Dr Preu, is called upon.
He's scientifically trained. A critical observer.
His careful examination helps to stem
The deluge of Kaspar's weeping; malformations

In both knees consistent with years of sitting
Legs stretched out in front…*this person, is neither*
Mad nor stupid, he concludes, *but has evidently*
Been forcibly removed in the most brutal fashion
From all intercourse with society and other human beings.

Kaspar Hauser is not a swindler. All the medical
Evidence published two years later confirms
That Kaspar was removed in earliest childhood
And reared in a secret place to which daylight
Could not penetrate.

News Spreads

Soon Kaspar's the novelty of Nuremberg, superior
To Herr van Aken's kangaroo and tame hyena.

Free public access leaves him little respite. But his
Good nature raises him above a freakish spectacle,

Invites the avalanche of presents that turns his cell
Into a grotto of toy soldiers, wooden animals, coins,

Clothes, pictures. The dress coats, waist coats suggest
Some wish to see him dressed above his cell-bound

Foundling status. He's fastidious to a fault; each
Morning glues all the pictures to the walls

With his strangely sticky spittle, arranges every toy
Just so, puts them all away each evening, takes

Down the pictures, places them in a bedside pile,
Gifts of clothes folded beneath his pillow.

There was nothing bad about him. I'd bear witness
To his innocence were God Himself to cast him out…

(Thus Hiltel, prison keeper, face aflame with
Indignation that there could be any doubt).

Interrogation

June – July 1828

Kaspar's passed to Chief of Police,
Mayor Binder. Interrogation starts.
Six weeks later, Kaspar's reality
Has so far broken through all
Surface hostility and suspicion

That Binder's thrown caution
To the winds. His report's deemed
Too full-hearted to be professional.
He receives a reprimand but is
Unashamed. *His strangest of all*

Strange announcements is unusually long.
One sentence alone, a tidal wave
Of unreserved wonder and affection.
Binder's never met the like. Such
Exalted innocence…indescribable gentleness…

Warmth…good-naturedness…aversion
To anything which would cause
*The slightest pain to man or beast…*is *free*
*From any bad behaviour…*complies *with*
Everything good. His desire to learn

(He knows about fifty words) is *quite*
Exceptional. Has an *unusual love of order*
And cleanliness; his whole *childlike self*
*And his pure unsullied being…*are *richly*
Endowed…with the most splendid gifts

*Of spirit, disposition and heart…*He's
Heaven-sent. *The community love him*
And regard him as a pledge of love sent
To them by Providence. Binder's Report
Is a lit fuse showering sparks

Throughout the land and across
The continent. *The Child of Europe*
Comes into being. A bright star
Begins to shine, and the perfect
Crime shows signs of unravelling.

Anselm Ritter von Feuerbach

President of the Court of Appeal
in Ansbach, Criminologist
and Instructor in Criminal Law
and foremost criminal lawyer of his day.

11th July 1828

Drawn to visit, he reports,
Out of humanitarian and
Scientific interests to see
This unique phenomenon.

Words which fail to convey
Anything of the inferno
Soon to rage within him
In his search to lay bare

This crime against the soul life
Of the human being.

Feuerbach's Visit

Kaspar's bare-footed, wearing
A pair of old leg coverings
And a shirt, as Feuerbach enters
With Colonel von D., two ladies

And two children. Six weeks on,
It's still open house day after day.
Yet his face is a picture of *trusting*
Acceptance and pleasure at seeing us.

The Colonel's uniform and gold-
Embellished helmet first hold
His attention, then the ladies' dresses,
While the most eminent and acute

Of all his many observers, drab
In black, fails to catch his eye,
Though each comes under the closest
Scrutiny when introduced. *Each*

Particular feature in turn: forehead, eyes,
*Nose, mouth…*absorbed with a quick
Penetrating glance while their name
Is repeated as if to seal the whole

Impression, never to be forgotten.

*

Continued over…

The room's small and clean.
And open to extensive views.
Kaspar blinks *vigorously*, frowns,
Turns aside to avoid the shafts
Of sunlight streaming in.

Feuerbach tries to elicit something
Of his past. What he hears is *such*
Gibberish…I could only guess. What
Matters is what's self-evident:
Eyes unused to sunlight, absence

Of all but the most basic concepts,
Preference for bread and water,
Difficulty in walking, ignorance
Of ever having been subjected
To imprisonment and abuse..

Only a person who had gone through
And suffered what (he) has suffered
*Can be like Kaspar…*Speculations
Founded on his *muddled, murky*
Gibberish, are of no account.

He who doubts Kaspar's story
Concludes Feuerbach, *needs*
Doubt Kaspar's existence. He's
　　His own living proof.

Feuerbach's Testimony

He had not yet seen the moon or the stars,
Did not know what winter was…
Known words were freely used
To cover a range of meanings:

The man with the big mountain
(A pot-bellied man). *The lady*
With the lovely tail, (one with
A trailing scarf). His thirst

For knowledge *surpassed all belief*
As also *his iron determination*
To persevere with whatever tasks
He had set himself. It *was deeply*

Moving to watch. Yet he still longed
For his quiet cell and the Man
With whom he had always been with
His deliveries of bread and water.

But that Man? *People good…Man*
Not wicked. Man not do me bad.
As though he's prolonged his life
In Paradise. There, no *pains*

Continued over…

In the head, no people tiring him,
No offensive smells. Except, here
He's learning, learning…Feuerbach
Witnesses *convulsive spasms* flitting

Like lightning across the left side
Of his face, triggered by his eager
Interest: nervous flickers building
In intensity as he struggles to keep up

With all that's assaulting his senses,
Challenging him to understand.
So he'll freeze, as one suddenly
Immobilised, staring sightlessly

As from a switch thrown to prevent
Overload, or lapsing into silence
Struggling to fit new word to known
Concept, new concept to right word.

So much to learn. When he's mastered
All that the Mayor and Professor Daumer
Know, he'll go home to the Man
And show him all he's learned.

Who is Kaspar Hauser?

Can Anselm Ritter von Feuerbach quite believe
His own response? Carried away in spite of himself
Like Binder whom he criticises for *his precipitous*
And…quite inappropriate public address? Yet he
Confirms what Binder says. He sees in Kaspar

The image of eternity mirrored in the soul of an angel…
Filled with childish goodness and gentleness which made it
Impossible for him to do harm to a worm or fly let alone
To a human being. And more: Criminologist turns
Theologian. For him, Kaspar's a living refutation

Of the doctrine of original sin. Innocence and goodness
Of heart was evident in all his doing and speech although
He had not the slightest idea of right and wrong…people
Were all good in his eyes…all beautiful. And how
Account for *his amazing love of cleanliness and order*

In one whose body was covered with *an accumulated*
Crust of many years of dirt? And as for his *extraordinary*
Progress: what takes *others months or years he learns*
In days, writes Feuerbach in September, recalling
The *gibberish* of July, now transformed to speaking
In a perfectly understandable and coherent way.

So
many
riddles.

Who is Kaspar Hauser?

The Party is brought to a close

But Feuerbach's no dreamer.
He's too aware of *the whole nonsense*
Being enacted around Kasper Hauser,

Object of endless curiosity, *exhibited*
In social circles or in public houses
Like some strange animal, subjected

To frivolous experiments (*a drop*
Of wine in his water; let's see how
He reacts). Why hasn't it occured

To Binder to protect his so-called
Beloved charge? Place him into
The sole hands of an educated man?

Someone *sensible*, like the good
Professor Daumer? Feuerbach
Brings the weight of his authority

To bear,
    and brings the party to a close.

2. *Professor Daumer*

A World to be Recovered

Where outer senses' knowledge ends
There and there only is the gateway
That leads to the realities of life…
(from Whitsuntide, Rudolf Steiner)

The good Professor Daumer.
Poet-philosopher. Exact
Observer; scrupulous witness.
Tutor to Hegel's children,
(His former school-teacher).

Now in his late twenties,
Finds himself face to face
With a human being
Like no other, as if a long-
Forgotten World had reappeared,

To be recovered, re-discovered…

Immediate Hostility

Some blaze up at news
        of Kasper Hauser;
Suspicious; scorning
        eye-witness reports.

They've never set eyes
        on him themselves,
Never stood face to face
        yet somehow

They know best; like
        Police Counsel from Berlin
Johann Friedrich Merker,
        the news, being so

Out of the ordinary what
        possible conclusion
Can be reached other
        than that expressed

In his published title: *Kaspar Hauser,*

        Not Unlikely a Fraud?

The Higher Dignity of Man

For Daumer, it's symptomatic
Of a mounting tide of scepticism;
Only suspect. An age losing faith
In anything unable to be explained
To materialistic understanding.

Kaspar's uncorrupted nature
Recalls and reaffirms for him
The higher dignity of Man;
Like Feuerbach, he sees in him
Something humanly angelic.

Pure qualities of *innocence*
And goodness of heart…the finest
Sense of morality and most
Rigorous love of truth; a nobility
And gentleness of being

Upon which *rests…all culture*
In the fully human sense. That light,
Still shining despite the depths
Of diabolical abuse to which
It's been subjected, will serve

To navigate safe passage
Through the hostilities ahead.

Georg Friedrich Daumer

1800 – 1875

Lives long enough to see
Hopes dashed, his worst
Forebodings realised.

Not only his precious charge
Murdered, smeared with
Calumnies, but Germany

Under Prussia, newly-
Forged, belligerent.
Heading…not towards freedom,

Moral greatness, national
And human excellence;
Rather, to being *the slaves*

Of the Prussian dynastic,
Military despotism.
Victory over France

Celebrated (on a hilltop
Overlooking the Rhine)
In towering bronze.

There the victory wreath's
Held high; there the Kaiser's
Set amidst his soldiery.

Hear the winged trumpet
Splitting the air with its call
To arms: no looking back.

Georg Friedrich Daumer,
Esteemed by Nietzsche
Who divined at the time that

What was being destroyed
Was the German spirit
In favour of the German empire.

3. *Recovery*

The Daumer Sanctuary

from July 1828

But first, recovery. From dark years of confinement,
Two months of freedom and torturing celebrity;

A curiosity on show; the incessant bibble-babble
Of visitors; fraying nerves increasingly disordered

From the struggle to keep abreast, hands trembling,
Sudden *spasmodic movements of a terrifying kind…*

But now, recovery. In the sanctuary of Professor Daumer,
His sister and his mother. The public asked

To keep away.

Extended Rest

Recovery? But first collapse. Extended rest.
All teaching had to stop; the headaches,

The beads of perspiration breaking out
On his brow, the twitching of his face.

Rest. From every white or bright object
That hurt his eyes, from every loud word

Or note struck on the piano, from every
Gentle touch that felt more like a blow;

Rest. From learning to walk, still a shuffle
Of inturned toes at constant risk from

Overbalancing. Rest. From the raw sense
Of feeling *breathed upon*. Rest. From a body

Unbelievably frail, weak and oversensitive.
He became so ill he could hardly stand upright.

Step by Step

After rest: recovery. First, hands
Not head set to work. Pasting,
Joinery, gardening *in so far*
As he was up to it. A few games
In the open air; the occasional

Luke-warm bath. And riding lessons.
These, with notable success.
The convulsive movements,
The trembling, from overload
Of premature exposure to the public

Began to subside. Recovery;
Meaning strict attention to his diet.
Sweet things? Abhorrent to him.
Spiced foods and alcohol to be
Avoided at all costs (*terrifying effects*).

Vegetable acid made him itch,
Meat induced feverish spells.
The Daumers proceeded step
By cautious step. A soup of water
Thickened with flour went down well.

So too, white bread along with
Milk dishes. Plain chocolate also.
Their scrupulous attention
Bore fruit: his whole appearence
Improved; within a month,

He was all of two inches taller.

Learning to Walk

Feet *free of calluses and easily damaged*
Being so soft, though the forced efforts
Since his appearence had left

Significant traces of sores and blisters…
One could plainly see he had been
Unaccustomed to walking. The struggle

To do so always left him *dog tired*.

Coming into Focus

With rest: increasing health and strength.

He mastered the ability to step without
Swaying unsteadily, wobbling or stumbling.

As he got into his stride the green blur
Of nature came into focus: perceptions,
Concepts, speech together advancing

Rapidly to the point of being able
To *converse without difficulty on any subject*
Within…the range of his ideas and powers
Of comprehension. Daumer was astonished.

His capacity for learning was *incomprehensible*
As was the reach of his memory *and because*
Of its wholly unusual strength, it appeared

A true miracle.

No less incomprehensible…

The acute refinement of Kaspar's senses. A single
Drop of meat broth dripped into his watery soup?
He'd be aware. Walks through churchyards

Were best avoided: he couldn't bear the smell
Of corpses. He could see in the dark well enough
To distinguish colours (dark green from black)

And had a most curious sensitivity to metals:
(Gold, brass, copper, silver, lead). Wrap them:
He'd tell them apart. Asked to describe *the effect*

Of something held in front of him, wrapped
In paper (a diamond): 'It's like *the diamond*
Of a ring of mine.' Bullseye! Sensed kinship

Of like adamantine purity for all his gentleness?
But then: there was that unnerving sense
Of the approach of others, the feeling of being

Breathed upon. Daumer himself induced Kaspar's
Most violent reaction by extending his arm towards him
When his back was turned. Kaspar, (well over

A hundred yards away), swung about, sensing
With alarm, Daumer's outstretched arm.

Lessons Resume

The year turns. His recovery now
So far advanced his box of letters
Reappears and feeding, watering
His toy horses, dressing them
With ribbons no longer claims his time.

Looking back, it's a watershed.
One of the longest strides
Into the World he's been denied;
And this time without headaches,
Tremblings, breaking into a sweat.

Yet he still could not distinguish
(As with his toy horses) inanimate
Objects from the living: a statue
Spattered with dirt: why doesn't it
Wash itself? A crucifix: why doesn't

Someone take down the tortured man?
And he still had no idea that grass,
Plants, trees grew of themselves.
And telling him was beside the point:
It laid bare his *adamantine* quality

At odds with the unreserved obedience
He showed to those in fatherly authority
Who told him what to do. Knowing?
That was his own affair. The green world
    Was made by man.

That Summer (1829)

Nature conveyed to him nothing
Of beauty, only questions, questions
As if they'd prise free an inner self
Which, (wrote Feuerbach) was like
An oyster glued to its rock. That summer

Kaspar shook free: *joy and wonder,*
An indescribable state of excitement,
Seized him on witnessing the seeds
He'd sown, beginning to sprout
And grow. So also, the starry sky

Flooded his heart one clear
Summer night. He couldn't tear
His gaze away. *That really is*
The most beautiful thing I have seen…
From that point on he looked

At the world about him
With different eyes, though ones
No less questioning. *But who puts*
The many beautiful lights up there?

4. *Kaspar's Awakening and Fall*

Kaspar's 'Paradise'

Man not wicked. Man not do me bad.
The Man, not separated out.
Part of a World of which Kaspar
Knew nothing in his twilight state,
Beyond his daily needs being
Unfailingly supplied: the jug

Of water he drained, refilled
Of itself in due course, the bread
Also, (shared with his inanimate
Toy companions); nor when rousing
From a deeper sleep than usual,
How it came about his nails and hair

Were clipped and he felt cleaner
In himself and with his bedding
Changed. Such the rhythms
And rituals of Kaspar's 'paradise',
Right and wrong as unknown
To his strange angelic purity

As gaoler/prisoner.

Separating Out

Rest, recovery? Daumer's devoted
Tutoring meant– Kaspar's Fall:
Touching down, separating out.
And then? Inborn good-naturedness,

Soft heartedness, that exalted innocence
Concerned for his captor's state
Of being, clouded over with
Darkening fear, mistrust.

Feuerbach, bent on bringing
Kaspar's captors to justice, needed
All that Kaspar had to tell. How
Could this be done without him

Waking up to thoughts of being
Wronged? Kaspar brought up sharp.

Question after Question

The more his inner being opened
To the World's beauty, the more
The darkness of his past rose with
Question after question: *Why did*
That bad man keep me locked up…

And never showed me these beautiful things?
I never did anything bad. Once more,
The uncontrollable sobbing. The blank
Darkness and threats that still might
Be in store for him. Mists clearing

To reveal sun and shadow; wonder
At a World coming into focus,
Sharpening the shadows of the past:
The cold reach of the motherless dark
Which had brought him up to be

Abandoned, submerged and drowned.
And now Kaspar, newly awakened,
Writing skills sufficiently advanced,
Lets it be known he wishes to write
His story down. It's the talk of the town,

And echoes,
echoes around…

⋆

Who now decides
    it's time to act?

Those in the House of Baden,
    guilty of dynastic crime?

Or Spiders
    with more far-reaching webs

Sensing their years
    of wrecking gone awry?

Progress Reversed

Recovery. But the first person still struggling
To make it to his lips, slipping in and out
Uneasily as though its inner resting place
Were too sheer, too insecure; the present,

A swaying bridge extending across a past
Of whelming vacancy liable at times
To rise and cloud his skies. As the year
Waned and the days closed in again,

Kaspar's blossoming appeared to stall,
Nipped in a touch of frost. Lessons
Became irksome. Daumer looked on
With questioning regret. Kaspar's

Remarkable sensitivites, the attraction
He'd held for wild things, had declined:
His own feral cat used to seeking Kaspar out,
Now passed him by as if sensing

He was fading into human ways.
Was it his own 'civilising' education,
(Wondered Daumer) including Kaspar
Now being well accustomed to a diet

Of meat? That *deplorable deadening*
Of his moral sensitivities, that tendency
To spin stories when confronted
About lessons he'd skipped…It was

Beginning to mar the all-too precious
Pristine image Daumer held of his charge.
And worse still, as autumn wore on,
It seemed the lengthening darkness

Stirred in Kaspar a new sense of being
Breathed upon. As if the awoken nature
Of his past were closing in on him
With some nameless threatening intent,

A suffocating sense of dread. Poor Daumer!
He'd never reckoned on the year's progress
Being set into reverse: first, Kaspar
Refusing lessons, then, huddled in his room,

Head buried behind clasped knees? All
His measured care, attention, self-discipline?
Yet Kaspar losing his footing, tumbling
All the way down to this? As if back where

He'd started: needing to be set on his feet again.
He felt at a loss: this icy breath seeming
To hold Kaspar captive froze up too
His own resolution: his warmth and will

To love, reassure, encourage, cajole.

Sunday, October 17th 1829

That morning, Kaspar had nibbled a walnut
And felt sick. Daumer had given leave
For him to miss the morning's arithmetic
So he'd retired to his room, intending to write.
He couldn't settle. The abdominal discomfort
Kept troubling him and a *natural need* made him
Seek out the privy downstairs in a passage
Adjoining the house. He'd been sitting there
Some time, when he heard footsteps approaching.

Peering through the screen, he saw a stranger
Dressed in black. Alarmed, he stooped to pull
His trousers up but his head showed above
The screen. The next he knew a blade flashed
And slashed his forehead as he ducked the blow.
You must die before you leave Nuremberg! It was
The Man's voice! Kaspar collapsed in shock
As his assailant made off. When he came to,
There was blood all over the place. *Mother!*

(His first thought, meaning Frau Daumer)
But his stumbling feet and his confusion
Misled him here, there, up– and finally down
Into the mothering dark of the cellar. By now
It was lunch-time and he was waited for. Usually
So prompt. In the end, the trail of blood helped
Search him out, *a white thing*, lying motionless
In the far corner. *He showed no signs of life.*
Pale as death, covered in blood. Only after

He'd been carried to his room did he stir,
Let out *an enormous groan. The man, the man!*
A powerful febrile shivering led finally to a *raving fit.*
He was *mentally gone for nearly forty-eight hours,*
Delirious, speaking incoherent fragments.
The slash he'd received, the forensic physician
Concluded was: *insignificant*. It could *easily*
Have healed in six days. But Kaspar's fragile,
Nervous disposition, needed three weeks
To recuperate.The authorities set to work,

Searching, asking for witnesses. According
To some, they drew a blank. Others disagree.
One witness reported seeing a man fitting
The description, leaving the house around midday;
Another spoke of someone similar at a public fountain
Seen washing his hands. And a few days later,
A *common-looking woman on her way into town*, said
A well-dressed man had joined her asking whether
Kaspar was alive or dead, and had then made off

After seeing posters asking for the public's help.

Assassination Attempt or Warning?

Was this a serious and determined attack
On Kaspar's life, or a warning? Putting
The fear of death into the growing youth?

Given the strides he'd made, his astonishing
Recovery under Daumer's care and tutoring,
Was this a brutal strategy to winkle him

Out of this all-too successful sanctuary?
Disrupt his progress? Keep him under much
Stricter surveillance? And find ways to turn

The tide of public interest and approbation,
Bring him into disrepute? The rumours
Already put about that he'd self-harmed

To draw attention to himself were grist
To this mill. *Only Suspect.* And some did.
Made it known, to Kaspar's great distress,

They regarded him a cowardly *sissy.*

All too much for Daumer

Now every ring of the bell felt
Like a violation of his sanctuary.

And the scar appearing across
The high forehead of his charge

Spoke of one marked out,
The indelible past rendered

Unmistakable. Yes, that deeper
Mystery! Outside the scope of his

Tutoring and the tolerance
Of his fraying nerves. Recovery?

Whose!? He would see his way
To continue tutoring.

But no longer as Kaspar's host.

Kaspar's Well-Wishers

The perfect storm echoed,
Re-echoed like peals of thunder
While Kaspar, in the eye
Of the storm's still centre
Lay, bandaged, resting
In a freshly whitewashed room,

Transformed by the shock.
It loosened the fetters of his mind,
His depressed mood disappeared.
(Baron von Tucher, soon
To be Kaspar's host). Mean-
While, strict guard was posted.

No entry. Even to the jostle
Of well-wishers: police, church,
Town dignitaries, the common folk.
It echoes on, that October storm's
Mystery. No doubt Philip Henry
Lord Stanhope (of Chevening in Kent)

Was also *well-dressed*, though not
In black and had no cause to wash
His hands in public. But it appears
His interest in the missing child
Went back years. Why was he
In town that day the storm broke?

(Though betraying no public interest
In Kaspar– at least, not then.)

5. *Winkled Out*

Leaving Daumer

Writing his story, the zenith
Of Kaspar's emergence. Then
The failed attack which
Put him in the fear of death.

And leaving Daumer?
A watershed. The summer's
Miracle, his new-found sense
Of the World's beauty blighted

By recurring melancholy.
At times, he wished he'd
Never been released. Not had
The misery to understand

All he'd missed. *A small tender tree,*
Wrote Feuerbach, *whose foliage*
Has been removed and whose
Deepest roots have been eaten by a worm.

No longer the Rare Sensation

Robbed of his childhood,
All too aware of his continuing
Ignorance, helplessness,
Dependency; in stark fact,

Unable ever to catch up,
Be respected for his usefulness
To society. His extraordinary
Sensitivities, the former power

Of his memory now *completely*
Diminished, and however remarkable
His truly iron resolve to learn,
His material accomplishments

Were little more than *beginnings*.
For Kaspar, leaving Daumer
Was like a 'coming of age':
No longer the rare sensation

That had stumbled, speechless,
Into Tallow Square.

Kaspar the Man

Targeted abuse aimed at his *inner essence,*
His higher spiritual nature, that was
The grave offence according to Feuerbach.

But whatever else his enemies wrecked,
The vital poles of Kaspar's nature
Remained intact: for von Tucker

As for Feuerbach: *an indescribable gentleness*
Coupled with *an unusual love of truth.*
His mild, even temperament once roused

In defence of *truths he decided were right*
And should be carried through, could not
Be persuaded otherwise. *Lovable hybrid*

He may have been, *in insight a small boy,*
In many things less than a child. Yet,
In his *dry but completely healthy commonsense*

He was a man!

Kaspar's Last Safe Haven

Baron von Tucher: his legal guardian,
Familiar with him since Tallow Square.
Words read like the colours of a rainbow
Spanning the darkness to come.

The purest unstained disposition…
          Good-heartedness…
Willingness to be of help to others…
          No natural wickedness in him…

And the shadows? The World about him!
Absorbing peoples' foibles, weaknesses:
Their insincerity, untruthfulness,
Pretence. Fertile ground for weeds

To sprout in him, *his spirit…still so soft…*
As capable of change and as receptive
To impressions as a twelve year-old boy…
A light-mindedness that could be *swayed*

To vanity and deception
but also corrected
With only a little supervision
and consequential strictness.

But the longest shadow was that cast by
The scar across his forehead: his learned
Proximity to terror, raising abject panic
At any threshold he perceived might
Threaten his security: a swim in the river,

A sail over the lake. Cowardly sissy?
Who could hold this fear of death against him?
Protested his guardian, *he who had just*
Begun to live and saw his precious life
*Already threatened…*Across his brow

The blade had etched the sign
of minus:
a life others had resolved
to wipe away.

6. *Enter Lord Stanhope*

A Present Help for a Soul Beset?

Demon of the English spirit? Or
Compelled solely out of goodwill?
Touched by Kaspar's dream
Of a stately home (as reported

In the *Bavarian Courier*)?
The thought pressing in with
Such insistent throbbing pressure:
His father's dream to be realised?

Chevening: site and centre
Of a regenerate glory? Kaspar
As catalyst? A modest work
Of his own winging Kaspar's way:

A Present Help…for a Soul Beset
(A book of prayers). An eccentric
English lord with time and ten
Thousand a year to hand (though

Wildly dispersed in lavish gifts
And gambling debts) but for all that
Meaning well? Maybe. And yet!
How difficult teasing apart heaven

From hell, being a secret agent
Continually strapped for cash.

Being a Secret Agent

In his country's service. Proven
Links to the House of Baden
(And its banks); life-long interests

In the occult; woven into elite
Connections Europe-wide bent
On preserving the power and

Gilded lifestyle of the Status Quo
In the wake of Napoleon's demise.
Hard to fathom what Kaspar's

Rumoured bloodline would have
To recommend it to stately
Chevening? And not just that…

The Message in the Bottle

Stanhope's network reached
To Friedrich von Gent whose
Unrivalled pen was proving

Indispensable to moribund
Regimes in need of propping up.
Close confident of Metternich,

Well versed in the political
Intrigues and secrets of the day,
He met Stanhope in Vienna

When news was breaking
Of Laufenburg and the Message
In the Bottle. Years before Kaspar's

Poignant dream appeared
In the *Bavarian Courier*, Stanhope
May well have been on his trail

Seeking his whereabouts on behalf
Of interests that did not
              wish Kaspar well.

The Message in the Bottle Resurfaces

Spring 1831

Sensation! Headline news
Once more. A Newspaper's
Fished up the story
Of the Message in the Bottle
From fifteen years ago.

Other newspapers have joined
The clamour. It's high time
This murky affair was
Unravelled and justice done.
All that earlier feverish

Speculation stirred up.
Questioning letters like that
Received by Binder soon after
Kaspar's release: "Is he
Stephanie de Beauharnais' son?"

Galvanised!

May 1831

Whitsun come round again and with it,
Stanhope, blown on the breath of the Spirit,
And certain news swelling his sails with
An almost indecent haste: Old Europe

In a ferment of discovery; *The Idiot*
Of Nuremberg to be restored to what is
Rightfully his: the throne of the Grand
Duchy of Baden? Stanhope's galvanised.

Wealth, family, status, to be marshalled
Into play, his own and Kaspar's dreams
At stake: the *Child of Europe*, his adopted
Heir-to-be breathing regeneration across

A sickening world from the dewy lawns
Of Chevening? Mundane orders also
Whispering in his ear to stop the Baden
Ferment boiling over? Both fair winds,

Combining happily for one of pious intent.

A Reception

In Binder's house. Stanhope, lanky
In ill-suiting green. But English
After all, eccentric and a lord:

Of practised charm, aura of wealth
And influence, and being a big fish
In a provincial German pond,

Who would not defer? Binder,
Scenting money, encouraged
The fortuitous arrival, but Tucher

Smelled a rat. All the fulsome
Praises for his safe haven? Then–
Why not leave Kaspar put? Why

The tempting vanity of gifts?
The gold watch, the promises?
Kaspar's future a cloud of dreams

In stately Chevening? Who was
Deceiving who? But Stanhope,
Fatherly hand on Kaspar's shoulder,

Mouthing 'my poor child', 'dear boy'
Soon had Baden's suspected heir in tow.

The Worm at Work

Lord Stanhope exerted a very adverse
influence on him (Baron von Tucher).

Vanity. The childish show Kaspar made
Of his gold watch! Winding it in public,
Putting it to his ear. Tucher could see
The Worm at work, the unsuspecting

Beams that Kaspar cast when 'the Lord'
Appeared, (*his guardian angel* people said,
Squirming even as they spoke). Stanhope
Announced his likely intention to adopt,

(Though he never did nor breathed
A word of any such thing to his family)
Left money for tutoring in English
And then was off. It was June. Tucher

Struggled on until November, but seeing
How deeply Stanhope had impressed
His mark upon Kaspar, that wealth
And money talk, resigned as guardian,

Knowing the moral cause was lost.

7. *Snared*

Winkled out once again

Kaspar, removed to Ansbach,
Set to a grind of lessons,
A kind of second imprisonment,
Squeezed in Latin thumbscrews;

What of the fatherly hand
On the shoulder? The dewy
Lawns of Chevening?
The future he'd been led

To believe was his? Kaspar,
Snared in appearances,
His trusting nature wide open
To yet more abuse: childish

Credulity to be exploited,
Small vanities, white lies
Amplified, turned against him
As proof of the fraud he surely is:

Continued over…

No heir to anything beyond
His own vanity and deceitfulness.
It hurts me very much, Kaspar
Confided to Andreas Hoffman

(Ansbach Councillor). *I know…*
His Lordship takes me for an impostor.
It makes me cry every night. I know
That I am not a deceiver…

What was at stake
        that required
                Kaspar's innocence
                        be proved a fake?

Why Ansbach?

Home of von Feuerbach, relentless in pursuit
Of Kaspar's cause, unravelling the tangled
Fine-spun threads that reeled in Stanhope
With such apparent haste. What better place

For Kaspar's proclaimed benefactor
To ingratiate himself, win the lawyer's
Unsuspecting confidence; (which he did)
Breeze in, keep abreast of his research?

Reassurance, too, for Kaspar: Feuerbach's
Passionate interest and fatherly support
Replacing Stanhope's, whose roving absences
Were more marked than fleeting appearences.

The Pace Quickening

January 1832

Feuerbach's foundational research is published.
It's headline news, even though holding back
On the politics of the wrong-doing. Later

Stanhope leaves Ansbach, promising to adopt,
Bring Kaspar home to Chevening. It's the last
Kaspar sees of him. He goes straight to Mannheim,

To Kaspar's 'mother'. Gives her Feuerbach's book.
Stephanie weeps on reading it, begs for a meeting
With her son. Stanhope promises to arrange it

But never does. Questions are resounding,
Insistent as drumbeats and impossible to ignore:
Now a force mobilised and on the move.

Kaspar's New Tutor

The *dry scholastic frippery* of hired tutor Meyer,
Is calculated to keep Kaspar in his place;
Of a piece with never allowing him outside
Unless escorted, tethered as if he's caged
Once more. Any non-compliance, request

For more freedom of movement is evidence
Of ungratefulness: to the Meyers
Who are looking after his best interests
And to his fatherly benefactor who, after all,
Is footing the bill (is he?). Kaspar can't win.

Any attempt at self-assertion shows his
Puffed-up vanity. (Who does he think he is?)
And if more proof is needed of the self-
Serving fraud he is at heart, that's garnered
By endlessly picking on him, accusing him

Of little lies.

Meyer Expects

How is Kaspar to thrive?
Meyer expects: diligence,
Discipline, hard work.

Does he (like von Tucher)
Find Kaspar's *truly iron resolve*
To learn? No! Lack of interest.

Poor concentration. Short
Attention span. Slow progress.
And what of Feuerbach's

Indescribable loving goodness?
Not a trace! Rather, *vanity,*
Egotism, self-absorption, illusions.

In short: what he'd suspected
All along. Nothing extraordinary,
(Beyond, perhaps, the practised fraud?)

Nothing very Extraordinary?

The image of eternity mirrored
In the soul of an angel, Feuerbach
Had enthused. And though

Kaspar's *loving goodness* remained
Undiminished in his eyes,
Much of the earlier expressed

Amazement, had come down
To earth: *there is nothing very*
Extraordinary about him apart from

The extraordinary circumstances
Of his fate… Feuerbach resigned
To this? Nothing more to be told?

Kaspar's soul and spirit stunted
For good? Nothing more to unfold?

The Rainbow Arc of Kaspar's Development

1.

The *Child of Europe, Idiot of Nuremberg*
Of the *purest, unstained disposition*
Suddenly appears in Tallow Square

Devoid of categories…no notion of God, no
Shadow of belief in any higher invisible
Existence…Is caught up in a whirlpool

Constantly at risk of being sucked under,
Drowned by the tumultuous surface
Welter of sensations and impressions.

Staying afloat, let alone wresting free,
Meant somehow keeping abreast,
Taking in, making sense of all

He was seeing, hearing, feeling, smelling,
Tasting. Two kinds of people he grew
To loathe in his early struggles to cope,

Doctors and clergymen! *The former*,
Because of *the disgusting medicines*
They prescribed that made people sick

Not well, and *clergymen* because *they*
Confused and frightened him with their
Incomprehensible blah, blah, blah. "They

Did not go away" he complained "*until*
I let them know I wanted them to just
Leave me alone".

2.

With Daumer's patient tutoring,
It was different. His sanctuary
Gave Kaspar the time and space
Necessary to haul himself out of
The whirlpool onto firm land,

And only then to help him
Appreciate there were more things
In the World than those grasped
By his five senses: the will
Inspiring him to learn, to form

Concepts, ideas, to think
His own thoughts. Kaspar's
Understanding, adamant
As it always was when it came
To 'knowing what he knew'

Began to awaken to such teaching.
It appealed to that *completely*
Healthy commonsense, to that
Which could be both conceived
And experienced as self-evident:

This inner being of his– and 'God'
Conceived as *the life in all things…*
The active spirit in the whole World.
It was a joy to him, a key to unlocking
The total imprisonment of body

Mind and soul to which he had been
Subjected, and which his physical
Release had done nothing to change,
Nor any amount of *blah, blah, blah*
However well meant.

3.

On the one hand, Kaspar's newly awakened
Feeling for beauty; on the other, the attempt
On his life and the loss of Daumer's sanctuary,
His truthfulness under suspicion for some;

And forever dependent on others: for his keep,
Protection, reassurance. Self-belief now lit
By that *active spirit*, now overcast, shrouded
In melancholy. The World's 'civilised' ways,

Its intellectual frame of mind, its animal diet
Dulling pristine powers of understanding,
Overlaying at times his innate truthfulness
(In *self-defence*, Daumer explained, *he could not*

Do otherwise). At no time could he ever really
Be comforted about his destiny, (Feuerbach).
What, then, of the rainbow arc spanning
Kaspar's short-lived development?

Was there the fabled 'pot of gold' waiting
To be unearthed? Kaspar's 'coming down
To earth' led him into the usual religious
Ways of thinking. So that in time his former

Aversion to religion transformed into *devotion*:
To God and *religious faith in His Providence*,
(Feuerbach again). Precisely how and when
Such a change found *access to his soul*

So in need of comfort, no-one knows.

8. *Kaspar Comes of Age*

1833: The Final Year

Faith in Providence? Yes! And
In the person of a *clergyman*
To appear as guide and father-
Figure at Kaspar's side.

Of like age to tutor Meyer,
And the perfect antidote
In kindly understanding:
Lutheran Pastor Fuhrmann:

Requested to prepare Kaspar
For confirmation as he comes
Of age. And helping to buoy
Kaspar's worldly spirits: he's

Profitably employed (when
Not under Latin thumbscrews),
As a clerk in the municipal offices
And of an evening, frequently

The invited dinner-guest
Of district president von Stichener;
What's more, invited to go
Dancing: how could he refuse!

Johann Simon Heinrich Fuhrmann

…by far the most attentive and sensitive
observer in the portrayal of (*Kaspar's*)
inner development
(Peter Tradowsky)

In Kaspar, Fuhrmann perceived
One who: *belongs to the sort of people*
Who are capable of anything when

Spoken to kindly, but who become easily
Confused by strict treatment to such
An extent that they no longer know

What they are doing…
They were to meet
For between five to seven hours
Each week for the next eight months.

Future Possibilities?

Fuhrmann's pedagogical approach
Spoke for itself. Where Meyer
Railed at Kaspar's 'lack of interest'
'Short attention span', he spoke
Of *hours of pleasure…blissful hours*

In lessons with Kaspar, studying
The Gospels and questioning
Religion. For Meyer, Kaspar's
Pious sensitivities were a 'show',
('Crocodile tears'). For Fuhrmann:

It is not easy to find a gentler, more
Tender-hearted, friendly and loving person
Than he. Like Feuerbach, he perceived
A *dissociation of maturity*: a mind
That had to struggle enormously

With the difficulties of his development
(Including *the affliction of white lies*
And little acts of cunning and the like…
To be found in most if not all children
Of his mental age.) Wounded,

Traumatised yet retaining
Elements of a childlike spirit,
A good, heartfelt innocent soul…No-one
Will ever achieve the transformation
That you have. Words to Kaspar

Hinting at possibilities seemingly
  Ruled out in Feuerbach's
    Pessimistic remark.

No Holding Back

Like Daumer, Fuhrmann sensed
Something uniquely precious
Was being entrusted to his care,

A sacred task: to prepare Kaspar
To enter a right relationship
With Christ. One (therefore?)

Likely to be ignored or given
Scant attention in most accounts
Of Kaspar's life: being of no

Outer significance (or simply
So much *blah, blah, blah*?)
For Fuhrmann, his first concern:

How best to engage with the person
In front of him. But in this case
Also, a felt need to keep records

After each lesson, publish details
Of the Confirmation, knowing
The suspicion and hostility

Kaspar's person could arouse.
To ignore (or dismiss) Fuhrmann's
Published witness would be

A conscious choice. Towards Meyer
Or Stanhope, he was the very soul
Of discretion. But when it came

To what he felt able to disclose
From his own first-hand experience,
There was no such holding back.

Preparation for Confirmation

The Pastor would make little headway
In engaging Kaspar with the teachings
And life of Christ, thought Feuerbach.
But the practice alone proved otherwise.

For Fuhrmann, Kaspar's previous
Hostility to the religion of clergymen
And his *dissociation of maturity* did not
Preclude a later unfolding of spiritual

Capacities. And what of the imponderable
Education that Life in all its changing
Circumstances provides? Wrapped up
In Kaspar's questioning objections,

He sensed *a soul thirsty for salvation*;
Gently encouraged him (given his
Declared faith in Providence) to persist
Along the path of transformation

Despite all that conspired to hold him back.

A Late Unfolding

Daumer's patient tutoring
Had given Kaspar the means
To haul himself onto firm land.
Now Fuhrmann's openness
To a possible late unfolding

Furnished another opportunity.
What was different, he observed,
About Kaspar's conventional
Religiosity was its depth and
Earnestness. *His tears flowed*

Continually at the telling of the story
Of Jesus Christ, especially
His sufferings and the teaching
Of redemption: childlike
Openness matched, however,

By an adult's refusal to accept
Anything on the say-so
Of authority: it went against
The grain of his nature.

Continued over…

This *paradisal soul* from far away:
Unwelcome arrival on an Earth
So far-fallen, as to seek his spiritual
Destruction; surviving to inhabit
Its state, enduring to recapitulate

Its Fall in his own short life,
Descend into its alien ways
And forms of thought, think them
Through, in the presence of
Heinrich Fuhrmann's rendering

Of the life of Christ; discover
There, a faith bedded in, arising
From the mysteries and extremes
Of his own experiences. *His words*
And gestures (Fuhrmann witnessing

Kaspar's eager responses
To the Gospel story) *displayed*
The deepest devotion: anyone seeing him
In these moments as I did, was filled
With amazement.

A New World

I feel really well, said Kaspar, *in the world*
Into which he has led me. (One so different
To that of tethered confinement,
Or the swaying bridge he'd had to cross
Out of darkness into blinding light);

While here: a new World within that World
(Or rather, embracing it?) That of
The *suffering Redeemer* and His restoring
Capacity to forgive. A World with which
Kaspar had appeared so strangely

Intimate, in those early utterances
Following his release. *It is a real comfort to me*,
He said to Fuhrmann, *to know that I am*
Not lost even when I am rejected by everyone.
(*Drive him away. Hang him in the chimney…*

Imposter. Deceiver. *Not unlikely a fraud*).
Claims repeated *ad nauseum* to this day.

Confirmation

May 20th 1833

Kaspar comes safely to harbour,
Berthed in the Chapel
Of the Swan Knight. The Pastor's
Teaching has brought Christ's passion
To the suffering mystery of his heart.

He came from bread and water
And now receives bread and wine:
This spiritual communion the zenith
And completion of his short life.
The Chapel's full to overflowing;

In festive mood, soulful, heartfelt.
As he kneels before the altar,
The choir sings: *prepare in me, O Lord,*
A heart that's pure…and take not
Thy Holy Spirit from me. The air's

Arrested, brings to those gathered
His exalted focus; *every lip moved*
Quietly in response; all hearts prayed
With him and for him. Hundreds say,
For them it is still a day of exaltation.

The Saving Mystery

If, like Christ's betrayal, Kaspar's murder
Was inevitable, the circumstances
Suggest it might not be accomplished
Until the evil that had worked to fashion
His spiritual death, had finally been
Displaced by Kaspar's full-hearted entry
Into the saving Mystery of Christ.

Aborted, that cultured peace he might
Have brought to the heart of Europe.
But his essential being proved its adamantine
Virtue; that *indescribable gentleness…*
That unusual love of truth, both bridge
And beacon to the future, our original
Innocence won through all attempts to suppress,

Corrupt, and, like a lodestone, finding
Its true bearings thanks to good-willed folk
Able to trust the evidence of their eyes
And hearts; and those central to his care
And education: Fuhrmann, Feuerbach,
Von Tucher, Daumer. Small wonder,
That among Kaspar's dying words,

Would be: *God gave me the best of people.*

Put out the Light

In the year without a summer,
When the Undead rose
To life from within the sunless
Atmosphere, to inhabit the souls
Of those confined, fantasy

Echoed a reality unknown
To them: The Experiment finally
Underway; to cut off an all-too
Special Soul from its birthright:
Its origins *Above*. (And not by killing

One so young whose pristine forces
Might soon find their way to Earth
Again); this soul was to be walled up
Alive: a living death, kept from
The light of day, the light and warmth

Of the human heart, until judged
Ready to be released into its own
Eternal unremarked demise, life-
Mission aborted and powerless
In death. *Put out the light*. And there

Stood Kaspar Hauser, crippled
Humanity, snuffed out in Tallow Square.

May 29th 1833

Nine days after Kaspar's Confirmation
He's bereaved of the fatherly oversight
Of Feuerbach. Someone had given him
Something, he scribbled on a piece of paper

Before dying in agony, convinced
Of being poisoned. He was in Frankfurt
For a meeting concerning this *crime*
Against the soul-life of the human being.

The matter was covered up until
Years later, when permission to exhume
Was granted…then revoked. *This crime…*
How close to home and Feurerbach

Unaware? Who better than Kaspar's
Benefactor with whom to share
What he dare not publish? So,
That compromising letter in May,

Setting out proofs (in confidence)
Of Kaspar's royal descent. And who
Better than secret agent Stanhope
To know the full measure of the threat

Posed by what Feuerbach could tell–
And the sobering consideration that,
Should the need finally arise, getting
Rid of Kaspar Hauser would be

Challenging were Feuerbach still alive.

Coming of Age

Summer to Michaelmas 1833

First, a long discussion with the King of Bavaria
Asking help to make it known that those guilty
Of crimes against him should not be punished.

Then, a naive and growing sense of independence
As he turns 21. He dreams of throwing off Meyer's
Tiresome constraints; visits former guardian-friends,

Binder, Daumer; toys with thoughts of returning
To the Daumer paradise unaware that he's as free
As a fly in a spider's web. And for how much longer

Will his enemies tolerate the notions now so firmly
Implanted as to his true identity and that insistent
Questioning hope that one day he'll know for certain

Who his mother is.

Kaspar's Mother

The unravelling stops, as long suspected,
At Stephanie de Beauharnais. *Beautiful*
Harnass! Strategic to Napoleon's expansive
Domination of Europe. Whereby Germany
Would unite with France in the union of his
Adopted daughter with Karl of the House of Baden.

Oh! Kaspar's mother! Napoleon received news
Of her new-born's supposed untimely death
Home from his own defeat in the winter snows.
How tangled his misguided genius in murder
And deceit within the House of Baden riddled

With dynastic rivalries! Death (or abduction)
Intervened to deny both of Stephanie's boys
Their rightful throne, her husband, poisoned,
She, as powerless as all of them. Stanhope's
Promised meeting failing to materialise,

Why not seek Kaspar out herself, visit Ansbach
Incognito, hope for a glimpse, at least, of one
Of her lost children? She fainted, the story goes,
On seeing him in the park: so near, so close,
And yet so far. How could she disclose herself

To him, knowing what would follow?

Kaspar's Murder

December 14th 1833

A few weeks before, Stanhope had requested
Kaspar resume lessons with his Confessor.
So that December morning, saw them
Immersed, verse by verse in the Parable
Of the Wedding Feast, *in most earnest manner*,
Kaspar resolved to be *a bearer of higher life*,
(One of the many to be invited. One

Of the few freely willing to respond?).
Later, a note to meet is delivered, promising
Information about his mother. The time
Arrives. (Four o'clock) moved on from
Whitsun to Advent. From Tallow Square
To the Royal Court Gardens. The Orangerie's
Deserted. No blinding light, no searing sun.

Snow's on the ground. A stranger emerges,
Hands him a purple purse to distract the swift
Action of the dagger, stabbing four times,
Upwards to the heart. He staggers home
To Meyer's unconcern (lying again,
Done this to himself; more attention-seeking…)
"Show me to the spot!" Kaspar manages

The few hundred yards, collapses on return,
Meyer berating him for *this most stupid prank*;
Clear confirmation of what he's known
All along. *I explicitly advised him against making*
Any more fuss, states his report. *That in fact*
He deserved a good thrashing. Three days later,
Kaspar dies wrapped in Meyer's shroud

Of calumny: *inadvertent suicide!*

Cloud of Doubt

Inadvertent suicide? Shroud the light!
The World's growing dark and darker.

Its promises *so various, so beautiful, so new*,
Now bring *the eternal note of sadness in*.

So Matthew Arnold a few years later,
Addressing his beloved as the World

Was darkening for him. Is volcanic
Winter to remain? So also the Undead?

What if, in time, we substitute for Spirit,
    Avatars of virtual descent?

The Testing Time

A holy light in the final battle
Pastor Fuhrmann had said
At Kaspar's Confirmation.

Now already the testing time?
Kaspar's dying was filled
With light and darkness. *Why*

Should I be troubled…? Yet he felt
Anguish, dismay. Ah, no person
Can endure this battle alone, it is

*So hard…*As the end approached
Hauser no longer had earthly cares,
Observed Fuhrmann, *his soul*

  Was concerned with the divine.

Why should I have anger or resentment?
No-one has done me any harm…

Words suggesting his embattled Spirit
Already
  slipping free
    reconciled and calm…

A Mysterious Person
Mysteriously Killed

Words (from the Latin) on Kaspar's gravestone

At the funeral and in words published
Shortly afterwards, Fuhrmann
Denounced rumoured speculations
Of 'self-harm'. Kaspar's life? Sacrificial
From its very start, *amid the mockery*
Of humanity. A beautiful life imbued with love,
Now broken off *hardly had it even begun*.

At his Confirmation, he'd asked Kaspar
To forgive those who had robbed him
Of his childhood. Now Kaspar
Had responded yet again, asked him
To pray for his murderer, had uttered
The words of forgiveness with his dying lips,
Died with no wish to ascribe blame;

Not a willed self-sacrificial death
(He had so much unlived life yet to live);
But one still true to his essential self.
Kaspar, *preserver of God's likeness*, according
To Karl Konig, refugee from Hitler's
Version of what Germany had become.
This *mysterious person*, from so far away,

So echoing-close in gentleness, love
Of truth and life, for whom *daily,*
Ordinary occurrences were miraculous enough.
In whose *placid, mirror-like temperament*
One might see reflected back whatever
Spark of that original innocence remains
Alight, a living part of us, in a world

Where crippling abuse may serve to darken,
Dampen, snuff out the wondering trusting
        Innocence of the heart.

Munich, 25th December

A letter posted to Kaspar
As though he's still alive.
Ten days in Vienna, Munich

Without sight or sound
   Of the headline news?
To Philip Henry Stanhope,

This makes a kind of sense:
Greetings from your godfather:
   Proof of his innocence.

9. A Matter of Urgency

No Delay

26th December

Once Stanhope's letter
Is winging Kaspar's way

(Signed: *from your godfather*
Who loves you with all his heart)

There's no delay. The intention's
Clear. To smear his godson's name

And sully his memory.
Bavaria's minister of the interior

Is the first to receive (and reject)
The insistent strident claim

That *The Child of Europe's*
Ill-won fame rests on an

Essentially deceitful nature.

A Matter of Urgency

The Count's dealings were not performed solely in the interests of truth…he must have had concealed motives…(Daumer)

Within days, Stanhope's
Seeking out dignitaries
Europe-wide and witnesses
From Kaspar's early days
On a mission to persuade.

Daumer's unsuspecting.
Still thinks of him as
Kaspar's friend. Finds
Incomprehensible the changed
Nature of his bearing.

In repeated visits, he tries
To wheedle Daumer and
His mother into testifying
To Kaspar's deceitful nature.
No ears to hear anything

They have to say in his defence.
Daumer doesn't know what
To make of it. But his mother
Does. *Can you not see*, she blurts out
To him when Stanhope's left

He is the xxxxxxxx.
　　　　It's unprintable!
For *murderer*
　　　　Daumer puts in blanks.

Stanhope's Last Visit

Daumer's mother has done
With deference. This time
She tells the noble visitor
To his face *not to spread*
Infamy on the memory
Of one who once trusted you
In childish faith as a fatherly
Friend and benefactor. To this,

Stanhope responds with
A red face and *it will not*
Harm him now. Daumer
Records what happens next.
All of a sudden he jumped up
And ran down the stairs
As if pursued by the Furies.
They never saw him again.

As if Pursued by the Furies

But why? Why these strenuous attempts
To seek out and persuade witnesses
To alter or retract the evidence
Of their hearts and eyes? Will winning
Their connivance calm his feverish

Unrest? Has Kaspar left an impression
So indelible, it requires such
Extreme attempts to be erased?
Ease the necessary betrayal, being
The entangled agent that he is?

In the pay of others, yet as much
Snared by the one he's been hired
To snare? Is Kaspar's reflected
Innocence too hard to bear now
He's dead and Stanhope's finally

Compelled to prise apart heaven
From hell? Spread *infamy on the name*
Of one who once trusted him in childish faith?
Furies from within– and from without
Now the murder's done, and there's

No time for anything but to stir up
Fog, blunt the sharp edge of further
Questioning, invasive investigation;
Undermine the need for the reward
On offer; plant the seeds for reasonable

Doubt to take root and flourish?
Inadvertent suicide? Most probably
The truth (backed up by all manner
        Of suggestive proofs).

Only Suspect

Like mud, Suggestion sticks.
Only Suspect and the rest
Will follow; rumour, gossip,
Like a rolling fog blanketing

The landscape of the lower self,
That low-lying indolence in us
That loves to parrot what it's heard
Indifferent to its truth. What lies

Beyond our comfort zones
Of the predictable, mundane,
Is a threat. Why else deny, dismiss
Pour scorn on things we find

Unfamiliar, unproven, or difficult
To accept? Fog creeps in where
Suggestion sticks, becomes a shared
Murk, a comfortable obscurity where

Clarity is clouded and living truths
Drained of life by all manner
Of contrary, suggestive proofs.

Kaspar Hauser

Who could be more abused? An infant, captive,
Childhood forfeit. Penned like some animal;
Sealed in sunless suspense. Faculties stunted,
Unable rightly to unfold. Released when
Deemed old enough and wrecked beyond
Recovery, the mockery of his destined Self.

Yet something of pristine purity remained
Beyond reach of all his abusers could devise:
Irreducible diamond, adamantine to its depths;
Or like the oyster's instinctive, suffering
Discomfort unknown to itself, transforming
The timeless repeating years into pearl;

Later expressed as compassion, wonder
At the World, a sound instinct for truth.
Paradisal being, it was said. It cast no shadow
Until released, educated in the World's ways.
Kaspar Hauser: never bent on seeking
Redress. Rather learning (re-learning?)

Faith in Providence and *the best of people*
    Within the Temple of the Heart.

Epilogue

Blood and Iron

Beethoven in a rage, tearing out
The page of his Dedication,
Setting Schiller to thunder hope
Across a Europe ravaged by
Imperial vain-glory. Forfeit:

That *finest sense of morality, most*
Rigorous love of truth, nobility
And gentleness of being
(To temper, balance, guide
The martial energy of Mars).

Evil steals a march on
Somnambulant humanity.
Europe's heart-centre traded in
For moral poverty: the rule
  Of Blood and Iron.

Europe's Child. Why not the World's?

Pristine innocence returned to Earth,
Sought out, like the Christ-child
To be eliminated, the consequences

World-sized. Where the mediating
Middle to reconcile East and West?
Kaspar Hauser, the missing heart-beat

Of his time. Was lost– and found.
Recovered, rediscovered, essential Self
Risen from the ashes of a haunting crime;

Freed in death to expand, ripple out
Unconfined by space and time.
Earth-Seed sacrificed to root in us,

(Who else?) be his World's destined
Future; grow that reconciling Middle
Wherever placed by destiny;

World's warming breath to thaw
The advancing grip of Satanic
Principles: all-powerful Control,

    And Death. Kaspar Hauser:
Europe's Child. Why not the World's?
   (His true identity unfathomed)

Notes and Acknowledgements

Words in italics where the speaker or author are not directly alluded to will be from the eye witness reports or writings of Daumer, von Tucker, Feuerbach or Fuhrmann as variously quoted in:
Kaspar Hauser, The Struggle for the Spirit (Peter Tradowsky 2012);
Kaspar Hauser, Child of Europe (Eckart Böhmer 2019);
The Lost Prince (Jeffrey M Masson 1996);
The Confirmation of Kaspar Hauser (Peter Selg 2024), or
Kaspar Hauser (Karl Heyer 2024).

Grateful acknowledgements to these and also *Kaspar Hauser, Where did he come from?* (Terry Boardman 2006), Jakob Wassermann's novel of 1908 and David Constantine's rendering of 1998 in his *Collected Poems 2004* as well as the plethora of mixed material on the Internet which gives a clear impression of the controversy this life continues to excite.

The account of the attempted assassination is adapted from Feuerbach's book of 1832 quoted in full in *The Lost Prince*. Other italics are to be taken in context, mostly highlighted for emphasis.

Page 14, *Mt. Tambora:* on the island of Sumbawa (Indonesia) A violent volcanic eruption in April 1815 *belched out an enormous mass of dust, ash and sulphur particles into the atmosphere. Thus the year 1816 went down in history as The Year Without a Summer, for the black sphere of material particles had cast a veil into the atmosphere thereby distancing the earth from the warmth of the sun*. (See *Kaspar Hauser, Child of Europe*, Eckart Böhmer pp53/54).

This led to huge crop failures and widespread famine in parts of Europe and also the north-east of America. In citing the bloodshed involved in the French Revolution and the Napoleonic wars, Böhmer comments: *Now from spiritual science we know that a natural catastrophe is not just a natural catastrophe, but rather an occurrence that has a correlation with the human realm, in particular with the moral failure of the human being.*

Page 96, *Put out the Light:* Othello's words before murdering Desdemona.

By the same author published by Wynstones Press

The Twelve Senses

Our senses: the means by which we come to experience the world about us and within us.

But why twelve, not five? Because viewing the world through five senses alone misses out so much of what we actually sense and experience.

The twelve senses presented here give us a far more rounded picture of who we are. It's an expanded perspective which better equips us to understand the world – to *see into the life of things*, as Wordsworth put it – and to be better prepared to see our way through the challenges and opportunities of the digital age.

57 pages.
ISBN 978-0-946206-95-7

Poems for Younger Children

During his years of teaching within the Hereford Steiner Academy, David Donaldson composed a wide variety of verses for the children of his class.

Most of the enclosed poems were originally written for particular children, but we hope this book will allow these verses to bring joy and inspiration to many more children and adults alike.

46 pages.
ISBN 978-0-946206-65-0

More Poems for Younger Children

This second volume by David Donaldson, originally published as *Promises*, contains a further varied collection of poems, composed during his years of teaching within the Steiner Academy Hereford. All of these verses were originally written for particular children, with inspiration from the wonderfully diverse subjects which the Steiner-Waldorf curriculum contains. We hope this book will help to bring joy to many more children and adults alike.

64 pages.
ISBN 978-0-946206-97-1

A Treasury of Trees

Trees express the life of the Earth in all its variety, fruitfulness and mystery, from ancient beginnings to our present time. These 56 poems reflect the author's life-long love of trees; they are verses of celebration, remembrance and questioning reflection, drawing on first-hand observation and experience as well as historical research and well-known folk traditions and mythology.

A Treasury of Trees is a rich and imaginative exploration of our relationship to the Earth and all we stand to gain by entering more deeply into its life.

> "*This tree hymnal is indeed a work of devotion in which David Donaldson sings, it seems, almost every tree in Christendom, but often doing so, too, with a pagan magic.*"
>
> Matthew Barton, New View, Autumn 2018

78 pages.
ISBN 978-0-946206-81-0

A Treasury of Plants

This rich Collection of over sixty poems explores the world of plants from a variety of perspectives, taking in the Earth's different climactic regions and the evolution of the plant
world over time, delighting in its abundance and vitality.

It includes many common plants which have come to be woven into our own folk lore and mythologies and also explores how our own human processes of growth and development as free, conscious beings, are rooted in and belong to the same unfolding evolutionary process.

> *"We should live life on earth the way plants do. They remain fixed to the earth, but they transform it and evolve it."*
>
> Omraam Mikael Aivanhov

> *"There are many riches here, and the poems work best where they take imaginative flight, as they often do, in a flourish and ferment in which facts, images and sounds coalesce convincingly, creating the same kind of living union in words that plants themselves create, each in their own unique unfolding and uplift."*
>
> Matthew Barton, New View, Winter 2020/21

110 pages.
ISBN 978-0-946206-88-9

Wynstones Press
publishes and distributes a range of
Books, Advent Calendars, Cards and Prints.
For further information please see:

www.wynstonespress.com
info@wynstonespress.com